My First Animal Library
Chipmunks
by Mari Schuh

Bullfrog Books

Ideas for Parents and Teachers

Bullfrog Books let children practice reading informational text at the earliest reading levels. Repetition, familiar words, and photo labels support early readers.

Before Reading

- Discuss the cover photo. What does it tell them?
- Look at the picture glossary together. Read and discuss the words.

Read the Book

- "Walk" through the book and look at the photos. Let the child ask questions. Point out the photo labels.
- Read the book to the child, or have him or her read independently.

After Reading

- Prompt the child to think more. Ask: Have you ever seen a chipmunk? Where were you? What was the animal doing?

Bullfrog Books are published by Jump!
5357 Penn Avenue South
Minneapolis, MN 55419
www.jumplibrary.com

Library of Congress Cataloging-in-Publication Data

Schuh, Mari C., 1975– author.
  Chipmunks / by Mari Schuh.
     pages cm. — (My first animal library)
  Audience: Ages 5–8.
  Audience: K to grade 3.
  Includes index.
  ISBN 978-1-62031-288-9 (hardcover: alk. paper) —
  ISBN (invalid) 978-1-62496-348-3 (ebook)
1. Chipmunks—Juvenile literature. I. Title.
II. Series: Bullfrog books. My first animal library.
QL737.R68S34862 2016
599.36'4—dc23
                                      2015027762

Editor: Jenny Fretland VanVoorst
Series Designer: Ellen Huber
Book Designer: Michelle Sonnek
Photo Researcher: Michelle Sonnek

Photo Credits: Alamy, 3, 6–7, 18; CanStock, 12–13; Corbis 14–15; Getty, 16–17; Glow Images, 8–9; Shutterstock, cover, 4, 5, 10, 11, 22, 23br; SuperStock, 19, 20–21; Thinkstock, 24.

Printed in the United States of America at Corporate Graphics in North Mankato, Minnesota.

For Joe—MS

Table of Contents

Getting Ready 4

Parts of a Chipmunk 22

Picture Glossary 23

Index 24

To Learn More 24

Getting Ready

It is fall.

A chipmunk gets ready for winter.

He gathers food.

He will save it for the cold winter.

The chipmunk runs.
He finds seeds
and bugs.

The chipmunk climbs.

He finds berries and acorns.

11

Chipmunks are tiny.
But they have big
cheek pouches.

cheek
pouch

13

Look at those cheeks!
They are full of food.

Time to go!
The chipmunk
runs home.

He will store
the food there.

Winter is here.
The chipmunk is ready.

He has a warm burrow.

He has food stored.

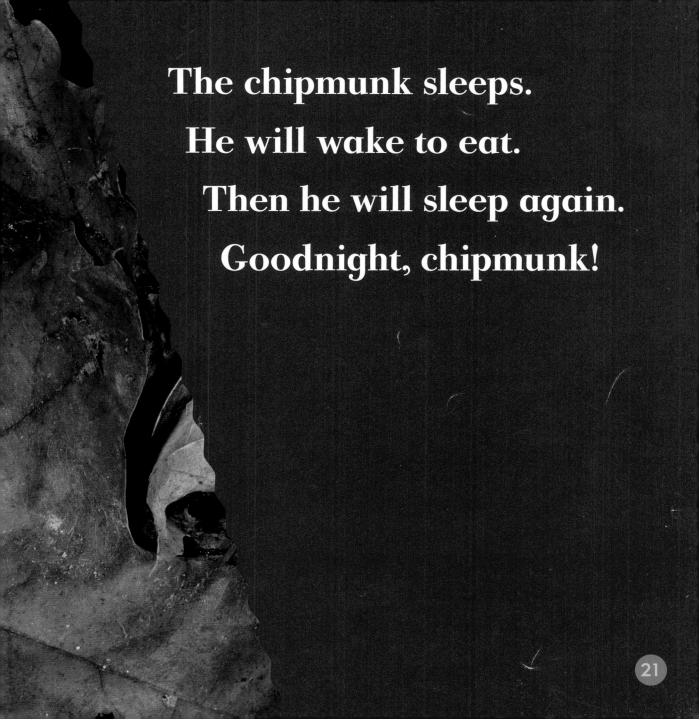

The chipmunk sleeps.
He will wake to eat.
Then he will sleep again.
Goodnight, chipmunk!

Parts of a Chipmunk

tail
A chipmunk's long tail helps it balance.

stripes
Chipmunks have stripes on their head and body.

cheek pouches
Stretchy pockets inside a chipmunk's mouth help it hold and carry food.

claws
Tiny claws help chipmunks hold onto food.

Picture Glossary

acorn
The nut of
an oak tree.

burrow
An animal's
underground
home.

berry
A small,
round fruit.

seed
The part of a
flowering plant
from which a new
plant can grow.

Index

acorns 11

berries 11

bugs 8

burrow 19

cheeks 12, 15

climbing 10

eating 21

fall 4

food 7, 15, 16, 19

seeds 8

sleeping 21

winter 5, 7, 18

To Learn More

Learning more is as easy as 1, 2, 3.

1) Go to www.factsurfer.com

2) Enter "chipmunks" into the search box.

3) Click the "Surf" button to see a list of websites.

With factsurfer.com, finding more information is just a click away.